Jubilee

The FIRST
Therapy Horse
and an Olympic Dream

by KT Johnston

illustrated by Anabella Ortiz

CAPSTONE EDITIONS
a capstone imprint

As a girl, Lis Hartel couldn't imagine life without horses. Horses were her playmates. She went on long trail rides with them, dashed around in a pony cart, and practiced jumping.

At age thirteen, Lis began competing in a sport called dressage. Dressage is like ballet on horseback. The horse has to carry out exact movements based on cues from its rider. The pair are judged on how smoothly they work together, like a single dancer.

By the time Lis was a young woman, she and her horse Gigolo had mastered the sport. In 1943, they became the national champions of Denmark, a feat they repeated in 1944. It seemed nothing could stop them.

But later that year, something did stop them. And it looked like Lis might never ride again.

Lis was a young mother when her world was changed. She had been having headaches and stiffness. She had lost the strength to care for her horses. When the doctor asked her to make a fist, her fingers could only make an *O* shape. When he tapped her knee, her leg did not jerk.

These were clear signs of polio, the illness sweeping through Denmark at the time. Polio could cause lasting paralysis, and sometimes even death.

Lis spent the next four months in the hospital, unable to move. When she went home, the doctor told her she would be lucky to walk again—with crutches. He said riding would be out of the question.

At home, Lis lay in bed, too weak to wipe away her tears.

"I'm going to ride again," she insisted. "I will!"

Lis was determined. At first, she focused on lifting her arms off the blanket. It took all her might. But soon she could push and pull herself short distances in a cart.

Lis's mother and husband helped her crawl—a grueling task that worked her whole body. The first day she could go only six feet before she was exhausted. She promised herself that every day she would go three feet farther. And she did.

At times, Lis made a game out of exercising to keep her spirits up. She and her little girl would have crawling races, giving them both the giggles. In fact, sometimes they were so busy laughing, neither of them made it to the finish line!

Although the workouts were painful, Lis wouldn't quit. She told herself that even the smallest improvement was a big achievement.

Bit by bit, Lis regained some strength in her arms and body, but her feet remained paralyzed. Even so, eight months later, Lis could walk with crutches. A few months after that, she was ready to prove her doctor wrong about riding.

"Put me on Gigolo. Walk us around!" Lis begged, but her husband had bad news. Gigolo had hurt his leg and could not be ridden anymore. Lis's plans were dashed.

"There's young Jubilee," her husband suggested. "She has a lot to learn, but she's calm and confident and smart. . . ."

Lis considered Jubilee. The horse was not elegant. She was tall and lanky. She looked nothing like a show horse. But Lis knew Jubilee's long back would offer a smooth ride—something she needed.

A new plan formed in Lis's mind. "Jubilee and I will learn together."

Jubilee stood like a statue as Lis's husband lifted her into the saddle. Lis could not grip the horse with her legs, so her husband held her in place while he walked beside Jubilee. A horse can tell when its rider is not secure, and Jubilee took extra care with Lis. Still, Lis lurched and tottered with each step. Afterward, Lis was sore and tired . . . and thrilled.

Walks with Jubilee became part of Lis's daily routine. Grooming Jubilee after riding was good therapy too. Each motion exercised different muscles—making broad swipes with brushes, bending to pick out hooves, plucking straw and combing snarls from Jubilee's mane and tail, and stroking the horse's velvety nose. Lis and Jubilee seemed to understand just what the other needed. While helping each other, the two were becoming friends.

Lis and Jubilee worked together every day. Rocking and swaying on horseback turned out to be excellent for rebuilding Lis's balance and muscles. Before long, Lis was riding on her own!

A rider normally guides a horse with their arms and legs, but Lis's hands on the reins were weak, and she couldn't nudge Jubilee with her knees or heels. How would Lis steer Jubilee?

Sometimes Jubilee went one direction when Lis thought they were going another, causing Lis to fall off. But no matter how spectacular the tumble, Jubilee was never spooked, and neither was Lis. Lis would not let a session end with a spill. She'd insist on getting back in the saddle.

Lis's determination paid off. She found she could use very small movements in her back to direct Jubilee. Jubilee learned to pay close attention to Lis's cues. Lis's light touch and Jubilee's cooperative nature were the perfect combination for the elegance of dressage.

Lis and Jubilee rehearsed fancy high-steps; they stepped out with flashy reach. They spun grandly on Jubilee's hind legs. They glided from one corner to another. They trotted, skipped, and pranced in place—backward, forward, and on the diagonal.

Lis got stronger, and the training was excellent for Jubilee as well. The horse developed sleek muscles, a beautiful arched neckline, and a majestic attitude. She was no longer lanky and ordinary. The pair had become quite impressive to watch.

Lis began to dream of competing again.

In 1947, two and a half years after Lis had been paralyzed by polio,
she and Jubilee entered their first show. That was just the beginning.
Soon they were winning shows across Denmark. Then their remarkable
performance in a Scandinavian event qualified them for the 1948 World
Olympics!

. . . Except that Lis was a woman. In those days,
Olympic dressage was limited to wealthy men
and military officers. Lis and Jubilee did not get to go.

The Olympic Games were held every four years. Over time, women's events were slowly being added. Lis hoped dressage would soon be one of them.

In the meantime, Lis and Jubilee kept competing. They beat Sweden's best duos. They defeated Finland's top teams. They began winning at the most advanced levels, including the highest, the Prix St. Georges.

Then came the news Lis had been waiting for. The 1952 Olympics would allow women to enter dressage!

But . . . there would be no separate women's division. It was the first Olympic sport where women would compete directly against men.

Lis knew expectations would be high. She and Jubilee had their work cut out for them.

They started training with the Danish Olympic team coach.

"Lift those feet, Jubilee!" he called, tapping the horse's back feet with his training stick.

Jubilee perked up. Lis perked up. They had to be perfect.

As she had done twice with Gigolo before polio, Lis won the Danish championship. This time, she'd done it with Jubilee—a tall, lanky mare never meant for dressage.

And now, Lis and Jubilee were going to the Olympics!

One hundred thirty-four riders entered the 1952 Olympics horse events. Among them were four brave women. Not only was Lis among this small group of pioneers, but she had significant physical challenges—and almost nobody knew it at the time.

Lis sat atop Jubilee waiting for the starting bell. She was so nervous, she nearly backed out. The hard work of rebuilding her body, the years of practice—it all came down to this moment.

But Jubilee was confident. The fresh outdoors, the cheering crowd, the loudspeaker . . . Jubilee seemed to love it! She was alert and excited.

The bell rang. Lis gathered her courage. She and Jubilee pranced into the ring and began to dance, the summer sun beaming down like a spotlight on a stage.

Lis and Jubilee showed the audience what they had, and the audience was enthralled. The spectators couldn't see any guidance from rider to horse. No nudges, squeezes, or flicks of Lis's feet, knees, or hands. The pair's dance looked effortless.

The crowd clapped to the music. Jubilee hammed it up. She perked up her ears, arched her neck handsomely, and lifted her feet even higher. She was having a blast! Despite Lis's jitters, Jubilee performed as easily as if she were in her home arena.

Afterward, Lis heard her name booming over the loudspeaker.
They were calling her to the podium!

A silver medal! Lis and Jubilee had placed second at the Olympics
with a stunning performance.

Surprising everyone, the man who placed first, Swedish army major Henri Saint Cyr, lifted Lis down from Jubilee's saddle. The crowd watched in amazement as Lis stepped unsteadily, holding his arm. He helped her to the podium before taking his own spot. Nobody had known Lis couldn't walk. They had had no idea that her touch with Jubilee was so delicate because it was all she could do.

Besides Lis's other firsts, she was the first civilian to earn a medal in an Olympic horse event. And she was the first woman ever to stand next to men on an Olympic winners' podium!

And stand she did.

Following the Olympics, Lis and Jubilee held exhibitions in London, New York, Toronto, and Paris. Lis donated the money she made to help polio victims. She and Jubilee continued to win many more championships. At the next Olympics, in 1956, Lis and Jubilee earned the silver medal again—and very nearly the gold. As the crowd's favorite, though, Lis and Jubilee certainly won their hearts.

It is satisfying to end a career on a high note, so Lis decided the 1956 Olympics would be Jubilee's last dance. After ten years of showing the world what they had, Lis retired Jubilee. From then on, Jubilee would have plenty of pasture time and relaxing rides around town.

The word *jubilee* means celebration, and Jubilee was named well. She was the inspiration—and the partner—that enabled Lis to reach her dreams.

And that's worth celebrating.

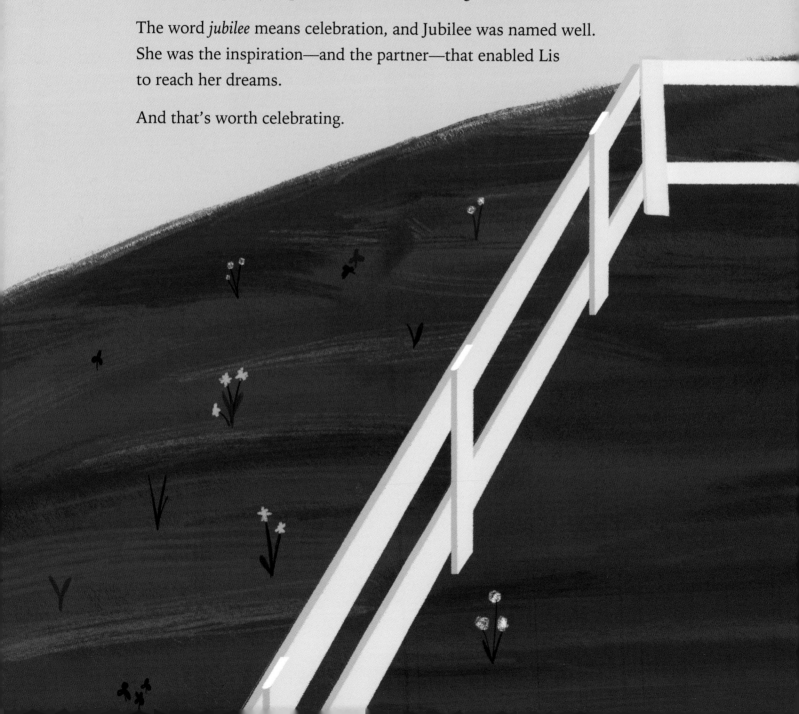

"Jubilee, my splendid brown mare, . . . a horse that has given me extraordinary happiness and many victories." —Lis Hartel, 1956

Author's Note

I ran across Lis and Jubilee's story while researching my picture book, *Railway Jack: The True Story of an Amazing Baboon.* Their story had all the elements I love—an ordinary animal from the dusty past that had an extraordinary impact on a person's life, and in some way, on humanity itself.

Major Saint Cyr's kind gesture is still considered one of the most touching moments in Olympic history. It brought immediate attention to Lis's story, and news coverage carried the full extent of her triumphs to the world. It also shone a light on her beautiful partnership with Jubilee. Lis embodied the healing effects of riding; until then, nobody had imagined that animals could help people in this way.

Although Jubilee died due to complications from an illness shortly after being retired, her legacy only grew. Inspired by the horse who had lifted her high enough to reach her dreams, Lis opened the first riding center for people with disabilities. Boosted by the Olympic coverage, the concept quickly spread, and within a decade, there were centers all around the world. The strengthening benefits of riding were recognized by the medical community, and a form of physical therapy we now call *hippotherapy* emerged.

Throughout her life, Lis remained involved with the Polio Foundation. She was inducted into Denmark's Hall of Fame in 1992 and to the International Women's Sports Hall of Fame in 1994. In 2005, she was named one of Denmark's all-time top ten athletes.

Lis was known as a charming and humble woman with steely determination and grit. But a successful dressage team also comes down to the horse. It was Jubilee's brilliant character that helped Lis dance on the world stage with her disability—and that has ultimately changed the lives of countless people who have followed in their stirrups.

Discussion Questions

- Animals have personalities, just like people. What sort of personality did Jubilee need to have in order to help Lis?

- Have you ever ridden a horse? Why do you suppose the motions of riding can help with building muscles? Which muscles can be helped?

- Why is it important to set many small goals instead of one large goal?

- What are all the ways in which Lis was "first"?

- After reading the Author's Note, describe what might have happened—or not happened—if Lis had decided not to enter the ring at the 1952 Olympics.

- If you were going to look up more information about this story at the library or on the internet, what keywords would you use in your search?

Discover More

All about horse therapy today, including where to find programs near you:

equestriantherapy.com

Video of Lis and Jubilee in shows and weekend riding:

youtube.com/embed/8FLZS0o62Fs?autoplay=1&rel=0 (4:18)

Selected Bibliography

Hartel, Lis. "As Young As Your Courage." In *Conquest of Disability,* by Sir Ian Fraser, 17–24. London: St. Martin's Press, 1956.

Jackson, Lorraine. "Olympic Girl Power: The Incredible Story of Lis Hartel." *Horse Nation.* November 17, 2014. horsenation.com/2014/11/17/olympic-girl-power-the-incredible-story-of-lis-hartel (accessed December 28, 2018).

Petersen, Nis. "LIS HARTEL." *Great Athletes* (Salem Press), 2001: 1019–1022.

Reuter, Coree. "Well Behaved Women Rarely Make History: Lis Hartel." *The Chronicle of the Horse.* May 27, 2010. chronofhorse.com/article/well-behaved-women-rarely-make-history-lis-hartel (accessed December 28, 2018).

Rottermann, Silke. "Jubilee, A Post-War Dressage Hero." *Eurodressage.* October 22, 2010. eurodressage.com/2010/10/22/jubilee-post-war-dressage-hero (accessed December 29, 2018).

Van Natta, Eleanor D. "A Woman, A Wheel Chair, and a Horse Named Jubilee: Celebrating Horses in Therapy and the Human Spirit." *The Equinest.* August 6, 2009. theequinest.com/lis-hartel (accessed December 28, 2018).

Vang, Rebecca. "Kvinden der fik sin vilje." *Politiken.* February 13, 2009. politiken.dk/sport/art4787914/Kvinden-der-fik-sin-vilje (accessed January 2, 2019).

Dedication

To all the dancers reaching for their own dreams, and the horses that lift them three feet closer. —KTJ

Acknowledgments

Deepest gratitude to my equestrian friend Elizabeth, whose input helped me describe horse care and dressage in ways that are correct yet easily understood. I'd like to thank fellow dog enthusiast Anja for Danish translations, and my friend and sounding board Nan, whose review comments are always generous and thoughtful. I am also eternally grateful for the care and skills of my editor, Kristen Mohn, and the rest of the team at Capstone.

Published by Capstone Editions, an imprint of Capstone.
1710 Roe Crest Drive
North Mankato, Minnesota 56003
capstonepub.com

Text copyright © 2022 by KT Johnston.
Illustrations copyright © 2022 by Anabella Ortiz.

Library of Congress Cataloging-in-Publication Data is available on the Library of Congress website.

ISBN: 9781684462551 (hardcover)
ISBN: 9781684464432 (ebook PDF)

Summary: Lis Hartel became paralyzed after contracting polio in 1944. Her dreams of riding horses and competing in the sport of dressage were shattered. After months in the hospital, doctors told her she'd never ride again. Lis tried anyway. How do you stay on a horse without using your legs? How do you give the subtle cues needed in dressage with limited mobility? With hard work— and an unlikely horse named Jubilee. After years of training together and creating a new way of communicating, Lis and Jubilee danced into the competition ring—and eventually all the way to the Olympics. Lis Hartel was the first woman with a disability ever to win an Olympic medal, and the first woman to stand equally beside men on the Olympic winners' podium in any sport.

Image Credits: Newscom/ZUMA Press/Keystone Pictures USA, 30

Designed by Tracy Davies

About the Author

KT Johnston is the author of *Railway Jack: The True Story of an Amazing Baboon*, an Amazon "Editor's Pick" Best Nonfiction for Kids. KT found history a boring subject in school, but now it's the passion of her writing. She has a degree in biology and conducted animal behavior studies before settling into a corporate career as an analyst. She and her husband are the parents of two grown children and live in Minneapolis. KT hopes to inspire others to be curious about our world and its past, one true story a time.

About the Illustrator

Anabella Ortiz is an illustrator and designer based in upstate South Carolina. From a young age, she has loved to draw and be creative. She studied illustration in Savannah, Georgia, and turned that passion into a career. Anabella enjoys collaborating with authors to bring their stories to life through illustrations that captivate and inspire. Having a positive impact in the world through illustration is her goal. When she's not creating, you can find Anabella at a concert, enjoying the outdoors, or petting her two cats.